D1519108

The U.S. NAVY

DAVID JORDAN

WORLD ALMANAC® LIBRARY

Please visit our web site at: www.worldalmanaclibrary.com
For a free color catalog describing World Almanac® Library's list of high-quality books
and multimedia programs, call 1-800-848-2928 (USA) or 1-800-387-3178 (Canada).
World Almanac® Library's fax: (414) 332-3567.

Library of Congress Cataloging-in-Publication Data

Jordan, David.
    The U.S. Navy / by David Jordan.
      p. cm. — (America's armed forces)
    Includes bibliographical references and index.
    ISBN 0-8368-5684-8 (lib. bdg.)
    ISBN 0-8368-5691-0 (softcover)
    1. United States. Navy—Juvenile literature. I. Title: United States Navy.
II. United States. Navy. III. Title. IV. Series.
    VA58.4.J6724 2004
    359'.00973—dc22   2004042795

First published in 2005 by
World Almanac® Library
330 West Olive Street, Suite 100
Milwaukee, WI 53212 USA

Copyright © 2005 by World Almanac® Library.

Developed by Amber Books Ltd.
Editor: James Bennett
Designer: Colin Hawes
Photo research: Sandra Assersohn, Natasha Jones
World Almanac® Library editor: Mark Sachner
World Almanac® Library art direction: Tammy West
World Almanac® Library production: Jessica Morris

Picture Acknowledgements
U.S. Navy: cover, 4, 7, 26, 29b, 30, 31, 33, 34, 35, 36, 38, 39, 41, 43; U.S. Navy (Naval Historical
Center): 7, 10, 11, 14, 15, 16, 18, 19, 24, 28; U.S. Naval Academy: 32; TRH: 6, 8, 9, 13, 17, 21,
22, 25, 27, 29t, 42. Maps: Patrick Mulrey.

Printed in Canada

2 3 4 5 6 7 8 9 09 08 07 06 05

About the Author

DAVID JORDAN is a lecturer at the Joint Services Command and Staff College in
Wiltshire, England, where he teaches Intermediate and Advanced Staff courses. He has
held posts at the Universities of Birmingham, Worcester, and Keele and has a Ph.D.
from the University of Birmingham. He is the author of several books, including
Aircraft Carriers and *The U.S. Navy Seals,* and currently lives in Oxfordshire, England.

Table of Contents

J 359 Jor

Introduction   4

Chapter 1
The Early Navy   6

Chapter 2
The U.S. Navy in the Nineteenth Century   10

Chapter 3
A Dominant Force (1900–1945)   16

Chapter 4
The Cold War Navy (1945–1991)   22

Chapter 5
The U.S. Navy Today   30

Chapter 6
Navy Technology and Personnel   36

Time Line   44
Glossary   45
Further Information   46
Index   47

Introduction

Right: A sailor "mans the rail" of the modern-day destroyer USS *Ramage* as the USS *Constitution* passes by. *Constitution* is the oldest warship still in service, having joined the U.S. Navy in 1797.

The United States Navy is one of the most powerful navies that the world has ever seen. It has around 375,000 men and women serving in it, and possesses around 400 ships and submarines. The United States Navy also has one of the largest air arms in the world, with about 4,000 aircraft and helicopters.

The Navy has always been a key part of the United States' armed forces, simply because the sea has played an important role in the nation's history from the days of the Revolutionary War (1775–1783) onward. To understand why this is the case, it is necessary to understand the importance of sea power in general.

As far back as ancient times, people made use of the sea as they sought markets for their goods. In the eighth century, the famed Vikings from Scandinavia used boats to carry war parties across the seas to plunder and conquer other lands. Countries needed to build their own navies if they were to protect their trading routes from pirates and ensure their enemies could not attack at will from the sea. The ancient Greek and Roman empires built formidable fleets for their day, and this enabled both of them to become great powers, with substantial trade links and the ability to deploy and supply armies on expeditions overseas.

In the late fourteenth century, adventurers from Europe sought fame and fortune by taking to the sea to discover new lands and new markets for the goods produced by their nations. The first major expeditions were taken by the Spanish and Portuguese, and they were soon followed by the English and the French. In 1492, Christopher Columbus' famed voyage led to the European discovery, exploration, and conquest of the American continent. The Spanish, the English, and the French started to build colonies in America, and the English eventually emerged as the dominant power after a series of wars between 1689 and the mid-1700s. Britain was particularly successful in establishing colonies on American soil and extended its trading routes to include the Caribbean. This favorable situation was not to last for the British, as the American colonists became increasingly unhappy with the way in which they were ruled from afar. This unhappiness finally exploded into the American Revolution, which in turn led to the birth of the United States Navy.

Chapter 1

The Early Navy

Right: The USS *Alfred* served with the U.S. Navy between 1775 and 1778 as the flagship of the first American naval squadron, fighting in the Revolutionary War. The ship is typical of the design of warships of the time.

The series of conflicts between Britain and its European neighbors that took place from 1689 onward were quite expensive. In an effort to pay for the wars, the British imposed larger taxes upon the American colonists. The colonists revolted, and as a result of British efforts to suppress them through the use of force, the Revolutionary War began.

The first efforts at building an American navy were on a small scale, with a few ships trying to seize British supplies. After the British bombarded Falmouth, Maine, the Continental Congress established a formal navy on October 13, 1775, and ordered two ships to be built. Thus, what would soon become the U.S. Navy was born.

On November 25, 1775, Congress passed an Act authorizing privateers to capture all British armed vessels and British supply and transport ships. Privateers were, as the name suggests, private ships authorized to go out and seize enemy vessels. The privateers were effective, and caused the British difficulties in supplying their troops.

The Navy in the Revolutionary War

The Continental Congress decided that it was necessary for troops to make a stand at Lake Champlain, an area of strategic importance between the present states of Vermont and New York, which formed a natural pathway between the United States and Canada. If the British captured Lake Champlain, they could

Left: The Continental Squadron, commanded by General Benedict Arnold, is illustrated here on Lake Champlain just before the battle of Valcour Island on October 11, 1776.

Above: A representation of the battle between the American ship *Bonhomme Richard* and the British frigate *Serapis* in 1779.

move on to take Fort George, then Albany and Fort Ticonderoga. General Benedict Arnold was put in charge of building a fleet on Lake Champlain, a task that was accomplished in just six weeks. Arnold positioned his fleet between Valcour Island and the New York shore of Lake Champlain, hidden from a British fleet that arrived on October 11, 1776. Arnold ordered his ships to attack, taking the British by surprise, but Arnold was outnumbered, and by nightfall the British had won. Looked at from another perspective, however, Arnold had been successful. The presence of an American inshore fleet meant that the British were forced to make sure they had sufficient ships to meet the threat posed by the Americans. This caused a delay in their plans, and meant that the British could not capture Albany, Fort Ticonderoga, or Fort George. Also, the Americans gained support from France, which provided some of its ships to assist the Navy in its battles against the British.

John Paul Jones

John Paul was born in Scotland on July 6, 1747. He joined the British Merchant Marine at the age of 12. He took command of his first vessel in 1769, but his crew **mutinied**, and Paul killed the leader of the rebels. To avoid trial, he went to Virginia and added the surname Jones to his name to hide his identity. When the Revolutionary War began, he joined the Navy and was quickly promoted. Jones proved successful, capturing many British ships. In recognition of his successes, he was given command of a squadron of ships, leading them from the *Bonhomme Richard*. It was while in command of this ship that he fought his famous action against the *Serapis*.

The next major naval action of note was by John Paul Jones in the *Bonhomme Richard*. Jones, a Scot who had **emigrated** to Virginia, had been operating in British home waters since 1777, leading a squadron of four American and two French ships. On September 23, 1779, he engaged the British **frigate** *Serapis* off the northeast coast of England. The *Serapis* was much more powerful than Jones' ship, but Jones fought skillfully. During the battle, *Bonhomme Richard* was badly damaged. (The suspicion has been that the French deliberately—and inexplicably—opened fire on Jones' ship and later claimed it was an accident, although some sources suggest that one of the *Bonhomme Richard*'s cannons blew up.) When the British captain asked Jones if he wished to surrender, Jones is said to have replied, "Sir, I have not yet begun to fight." Although his ship was now beginning to sink, Jones kept on fighting. His gunners damaged the mast on *Serapis*, and the British captain panicked and surrendered. The *Bonhomme Richard* sank two days later, and Jones transferred to *Serapis* and led his squadron from there instead. This famous action occurred at a time when the course of the war was turning in favor of the Americans, but it would be some time before independence was won.

Right: The U.S. frigate *Philadelphia* burns after being set on fire on February 16, 1804, by Lieutenant Stephen Decatur and his men, in an attempt to prevent its use by Barbary pirates who had captured the vessel.

By 1780, the Revolutionary War had turned in the Americans' favor. The British public was tired of the war and began to demand an end to the conflict. The defeat of British troops at the Battle of Yorktown on October 19, 1781 marked the beginning of the end. The American success was further aided when French allies used their fleet to prevent British ships from entering Chesapeake Bay. This meant that British forces in America could not be supplied, and as a result their defeat was inevitable. This prompted the British to seek a peace settlement. On September 3, 1783, a peace treaty was signed in Paris, and the British recognized an independent United States. This had a negative effect on the Continental Navy, however, since people felt that the end of the war meant that a navy was no longer needed. The ships were all sold, and the United States was left without a naval force.

This led to serious consequences for the newly independent nation, since the lack of a navy meant that American trading routes could be attacked by foreign powers. A small navy was created in response, and over the next 30 years, found itself fighting against Barbary pirates off the north African coast and against the French in The Undeclared War (also called The Quasi-War) of 1798. The Quasi-War was essentially an undeclared naval war between the United States and France. The French Revolution (1789–99) saw the fledgling French republic attempting to expand its political and economic interests abroad. In particular, conflicts arose in the Caribbean between France and the fleets of Britain, Spain, and the Netherlands. These conflicts also interfered

Below: USS *Constitution* defeats HMS *Guerriere* on August 19, 1812. The War of 1812 was inconclusive, but it persuaded Congress to increase spending on the navy so that it would be better equipped to fight wars in the future.

with U.S. trade routes and dragged the United States into the fighting. With France in political chaos, and its new government claiming that the U.S. had reneged on earlier treaties, French privateers began to seize U.S. ships trading with their British enemies.

The British practice of impressment, the seizure of American seamen for service in the British navy, led Congress to declare war on Britain in 1812. This was perhaps an unwise decision, since the British had a much larger fleet and could **blockade** American ports. Despite notable victories over the British fleets in a number of skirmishes when British and American vessels encountered one another, the war ended in a draw. Congress was convinced that a stronger navy was required, but the navy grew only modestly over the next 50 years.

One of the most notable uses of naval power during the first half of the nineteenth century came when Commodore Matthew Perry sailed to Japan to demand that the Japanese emperor open his ports and allow U.S. merchants to trade. Perry arrived in Japan in July 1853 and presented the U.S. demands to the Japanese. He returned in 1854 to conclude the negotiations. In March 1854, the Treaty of Kanagawa opened Japan to foreign trade, marking a clear success for U.S. naval power.

The Civil War and Beyond

The Civil War (1861–1865) saw considerable use of ships by the warring parties, particularly the Union side. As part of its war effort, the Union sought to deny supplies to the Confederacy. It also hoped to stop the Confederates from trading with other countries, damaging the Confederate economy and making it more difficult for them to continue the war. The Navy was given the task of blockading the Southern coast, and proved extremely successful in reducing the ability of the Confederacy to export goods and bring in much-needed supplies from overseas, despite Confederate attempts to break the blockade using fast, purpose-built ships known as blockade runners.

Although Confederate naval units fought courageously during the conflict, they could do little to overcome the larger Union navy. When the war ended, the U.S. Navy had around 700 ships in service, but by 1880, the Navy had been reduced to just 48 vessels. The reason for this decline was that the nation did not have the

Matthew Calbraith Perry

Born in 1789, Matthew Perry joined the Navy at age 15. He is best known for opening links with Japan after his two missions to the country in 1853 and 1854, but Perry was also responsible for some other important developments within the U.S. Navy. He oversaw the construction of the Navy's first steam-powered ship, established a naval apprentice program, and organized a naval engineer corps. He also played a major part in developing the first course of instruction at the Naval Academy at Annapolis.

Left: Commodore Matthew Perry is seen here transferring his command to the USS *Niagara* after the destruction of his flagship USS *Lawrence* in the battle of Lake Erie on September 10, 1813. Despite this setback, Perry oversaw the defeat of British ships that had been blockading Detroit.

Above: The ironclad Confederate ship *Virginia* (foreground) and the USS *Monitor* trade fire during their battle on March 9, 1862.

money needed to maintain a strong force. The Civil War had left the country in debt, and the cost of rebuilding the South was enormous. As the United States rebuilt, however, its **economy** improved. By the early 1880s, American businessmen wished to trade overseas and began demanding a strong navy to protect U.S. interests. The U.S. Navy was expanded over the next decade, and was put to the test in 1898, when the United States went to war with Spain.

In 1895, Spain's colonies included Puerto Rico and Cuba in the Caribbean, and the Philippines in the Pacific. Both Cuba and the Philippines wanted independence, and the U.S. public was appalled at stories of Spanish **atrocities** toward their colonists. The American people demanded that their government do something to help the Cubans. Anger toward Spain increased throughout 1897, and reached its peak when the USS *Maine* was destroyed in an explosion in Havana Harbor. It is still not clear what caused the explosion, but the American people blamed Spain, and popular opinion helped push the nation toward war.

At this time, the U.S. government was aware that the United States needed to have access to more markets for its manufactured goods. It was difficult to do this properly when other countries prevented free trade and open competition in their colonies, so it was in the United States' interests to try to end Spain's occupation of both Cuba and the Philippines. This step would also make sure that trade routes between the United States and China could not be threatened by another naval power. The war with Spain, while lasting only four months, led to an increased U.S. presence in both the Caribbean and South Pacific and helped fuel the growth of the United States into an expanding global power. The Spanish-American War also marked the last major test of the U.S. Navy in the 1800s. Many more challenges, however, were to face it in the twentieth century.

Below: The funeral procession in Havana, Cuba, for sailors killed when the USS *Maine* was destroyed in Havana Harbor in 1897.

Right: A recruiting poster from the early years of the twentieth century. Several posters like this were issued between 1900 and 1917 in an attempt to ensure the growing Navy had enough manpower.

YOUNG MEN WANTED FOR U.S. NAVY.

PAY $17^{60} TO $77^{00} PER MONTH ᴬᴺᴰ ALLOWANCES. BOARD, LODGING, MEDICAL ATTENDANCE FIRST OUTFIT OF UNIFORM FREE.

AN OPPORTUNITY FOR

The twentieth century was a time of great challenges for the U.S. Navy. In the aftermath of the war with Spain, the Navy continued to expand, enjoying considerable public support. The British launched a revolutionary new battleship, the HMS *Dreadnought*, in 1906, and this design made existing battleships obsolete thanks to its advanced construction, speed, and power. The U.S. Navy immediately began building similar battleships, and by the time that President Theodore Roosevelt left office in 1909, the U.S. Navy was the dominant naval force in the Western Hemisphere, and was rapidly becoming a major power in the Pacific.

The Navy continued to evolve at an impressive rate. Experimental work with submarines continued, while the airplane began to spark interest among senior officers. It was realized that airplanes would be useful in locating enemy forces and directing gunfire from battleships. The technology of the day was quite limited, but it was not long before a major war helped drive forward the development of naval aircraft and ships to carry them. The war in question was World War I.

World War I

Although World War I began in 1914, the United States did not enter the war until 1917, after Germany began unrestricted submarine warfare in an attempt to stop the flow of supplies to the Allies. In other words, German submarines were no longer limiting their attacks to their enemies' warships. President Woodrow Wilson declared war against Germany in April 1917, and immediately sent the Navy to assist the British in stopping the German submarines, also known as U-boats. U.S. destroyers played an important part in helping to defeat the submarine attacks. By the summer of 1918, British, French, and newly arrived

Theodore Roosevelt

Theodore Roosevelt first came to prominence as Assistant Secretary to the Navy in 1897, and was an enthusiastic supporter of sea power. He became president after William McKinley was assassinated in 1901, and remained convinced that the United States should maintain a strong navy, ensuring that funding was available to achieve this aim.

Airplanes at Sea

In 1910, a Curtiss biplane flown by Eugene Ely took off from a specially fitted platform on the cruiser *Birmingham* while it was at anchor in Hampton Roads, Virginia. Further flights were made, including a landing using ropes stretched across the improvised "flight deck" on board the *Birmingham*. Although Ely had shown that landings were possible, they were extremely difficult to achieve, and development turned toward floatplanes that could take off and land from the surface of the sea. This marked the first steps in naval aviation. The British built the first aircraft carrier, but the U.S. Navy took the lead in the 1930s. During World War II, the aircraft carrier became the dominant weapon at sea.

Right: Eugene Ely makes the first take-off by an airplane from the deck of a ship on November 14, 1910. The ship, USS *Birmingham*, had a specially built platform.

U.S. troops were driving the German armies out of France. Germany surrendered on November 11, 1918.

The end of the war was followed by a desire to avoid another war on the same scale. As a result, nations sought to disarm. The United States participated in this process, and the Navy was cut back. The only solid development for the Navy during this time was that it obtained its first aircraft carriers, which enabled it to experiment with ways of using aircraft in wartime. The Navy's

Left: The USS *Covington* sinks off Brest, France, on July 2, 1918. The ship had been torpedoed by a German U-boat the previous day and was under tow. It sank before it could reach the safety of a port.

fortunes improved when Franklin D. Roosevelt became president, since he saw a large shipbuilding program as a means of reducing unemployment during the Great Depression. Roosevelt also wanted to increase the size of the Navy because of the threat posed by Japan. The rise of Adolf Hitler and the Nazi party in Germany also increased the risk of war, with both Germany and Japan building large armed forces.

World War II

On September 1, 1939, Germany invaded Poland. Two days later, Britain and France declared war on Germany. The United States was again a neutral party in the conflict, but Roosevelt was sympathetic to the British and French causes since they were **democracies** fighting a **dictatorship**. To protect U.S. neutrality, Roosevelt set up a "neutrality zone," patrolled by the Navy, which was to ensure that warships from the warring countries did not attack U.S. shipping. To help the British, Roosevelt and British Prime Minister Winston Churchill agreed to a deal called "Lend-Lease" in September 1940. The U.S. Navy lent

50 **destroyers** to the British to help them fight German submarines, while the British leased land bases to the United States in a variety of locations around the world, including Ascension Island in the Atlantic Ocean and Jamaica in the Caribbean. Roosevelt also increased the size of the neutrality zone, and by the fall of 1941, U.S. ships were fighting German submarines in what was effectively an undeclared war.

Although Germany was a major concern, Roosevelt was also worried about Japan because of its campaign of aggression against China. On December 7, 1941, the Japanese used their aircraft carriers to launch a surprise attack on the Navy base at Pearl Harbor in Hawaii. The United States immediately declared war on Japan, which was followed by a declaration of war against the United States by Germany and its ally, Italy.

The U.S. Navy now found itself fighting in both the Pacific and the Atlantic Oceans. In the Atlantic, the Navy's role was similar to that in World War I, as it hunted down German submarines to prevent them from sinking Allied ships. By the middle of 1943, the German submarine threat had been defeated, and the Allies began to concentrate on invading Europe to liberate the countries Hitler occupied. U.S. battleships used their guns to bombard German fortifications, while a host of landing craft put men, tanks, and equipment onto the invasion beaches. Within a matter of months, most of the Allied armies had moved toward Germany. On May 8, 1945, the Germans surrendered.

In the Pacific, the Navy played an even greater part in the final victory. After the Japanese enjoyed early successes, they were badly beaten at the Battle of Midway in June 1942. After this battle, the U.S. Navy played an essential part in the drive to defeat Japan. Submarines wreaked havoc on Japanese shipping, while fighters and bombers from aircraft carriers sank numerous ships, destroyed many Japanese aircraft, and inflicted serious casualties on Japanese land forces. The Navy carried out amphibious operations as part of the "island hopping" campaign, which saw U.S. troops capture many of the islands seized by the Japanese, and then move on to islands close to the Japanese homeland, such as Okinawa and Iwo Jima. Japan was almost totally defeated, but struggled on until the United States compelled its surrender through the use of two atomic bombs in August 1945. To defeat Japan, the U.S. Navy became the most powerful navy in the world, a position that it has not relinquished to date.

Aircraft Carriers in the Pacific

After the attack on Pearl Harbor, the U.S. Navy began a massive program of ship-building to provide aircraft carriers. Since the Pacific is such a large ocean, the Navy was vitally important in winning the war. The first strike against Japan was launched from the carrier USS *Hornet* in 1942. In June 1942, the U.S. Navy won a major victory over the Japanese at the Battle of Midway. Carrier-borne aircraft sank four Japanese aircraft carriers, a blow from which Japan never recovered. The use of carrier-based aircraft was of great significance. U.S. naval aircraft sank large amounts of Japanese shipping and inflicted serious defeats on the Japanese air forces, particularly at the Marianas Islands in 1944. Aircraft were used to support the forces landing on Japanese-held islands, both by attacking Japanese strongpoints and by ensuring that the Japanese air forces could not attack U.S. troops.

Left: A group of U.S. Navy aviators being briefed by their commanding officer in 1944. The picture was probably staged for the camera, since such briefings usually took place inside the ship rather than on the noisy flight deck.

Right: A pair of U.S. Navy special forces commandos, known as SEALs (Sea, Air, and Land) on a beach reconnaissance training mission.

With the end of World War II, it was assumed that a strong military was no longer required since there was no obvious threat to the United States. As a result, the U.S. Navy was dramatically reduced in size (although it was still larger than any other nation's navy). Its operating budget dropped, and orders for ships were canceled. More ships were retired from service into the reserve, and even more were scrapped. Confidence that the world had returned to peace, however, was shattered when it became clear that the United States and the Soviet Union were not going to be able to resolve their differences. It seemed as if the Soviets wished to spread their **communist** system of government, something that the United States was determined to stop. Tensions between the two led to a period of confrontation between the United States and the Soviet Union known as the Cold War. It was called this because relations often came to the brink of war without actual fighting taking place. By 1949, the threat posed by the Soviet Union was judged serious enough to merit the creation of a defensive military alliance between the United States, Canada, Britain, and other European nations. The North Atlantic Treaty Organization (NATO) was formed as a result, and the U.S. Navy was given a key role in keeping open the sea lanes between North America and Europe.

The Korean War

In 1950, communist North Korea invaded South Korea in an attempt to unify the partitioned Korean peninsula under communist rule. As U.S. troops were in South Korea advising the government and South Korean armed forces, the United States was involved in the fighting almost immediately. The attack on South Korea was condemned by the United Nations, which authorized military action to beat off the communist invasion, and the United States played the dominant role in the war that followed. The North Koreans drove back U.S. and South Korean troops until they held just a small section of South Korea around the port of Pusan. Navy ships used their guns to provide fire support for the defenders of the Pusan perimeter, while the one available aircraft carrier launched its airplanes to carry out strikes against a variety of North Korean targets, which helped bring the communist advance to a halt.

More Navy ships, including carriers, were rushed to Korean waters, and then, on September 15, 1950, a daring amphibious assault was launched at the Korean

Right: The battleship USS *Missouri* fires a salvo of shells against a target in North Korea in October 1950. *Missouri* remained in service with the U.S. Navy until the early 1990s.

port of Inchon. This was well behind North Korean lines, and enabled the United States and other United Nations (U.N.) forces to attack the communists from the rear. The North Koreans retreated in confusion and were driven back across the border. As they went, they were harassed by carrier-based aircraft and naval gunfire. U.N. forces then crossed into North Korea, seeking to completely defeat the communists, which caused communist China to enter the war. A huge number of Chinese troops were deployed to drive the U.S. and U.N. forces back across the border. Once again, carrier aircraft played a vital role in supporting troops on the ground. The war settled into a stalemate, and a truce was eventually signed in 1953. Both sides had ended up virtually where they started.

The Vietnam War

The Navy resumed exercises with friendly navies for the rest of the 1950s and the early 1960s. By 1964, however, the United States was on the brink of another war, this time in a then little-known country called Vietnam. Vietnam had won independence from France in 1954 and been divided into two states as part of the initial phase of the peace process. The communist government in North Vietnam wanted to take over South Vietnam to unify the country under its control. The U.S. administration feared that if this happened, neighboring nations would fall to communism as well. As a result, the United States supported South Vietnam, sending military advisors to train the South's armed services.

On August 4, 1964, North Vietnamese patrol boats attacked the USS *Maddox* as it patrolled the Gulf of Tonkin, off the coast of North Vietnam. In retaliation, President Lyndon Johnson ordered carrier-based aircraft to attack the North Vietnamese torpedo boat bases. This began a long and painful U.S. commitment to Vietnam. More and more U.S. troops were poured into the country, until by 1969, there were 543,000 American service personnel in Vietnam, and the war was costing $30 billion each year. The most visible efforts by the U.S. Navy occurred in the form of air strikes launched from carriers against targets in North Vietnam and against the Viet Cong (communist

Below: A Vought F-8 Crusader of Navy Fighter Squadron 111 launches from the deck of the aircraft carrier USS *Oriskany* during the Vietnam War.

guerrillas fighting U.S. and South Vietnamese forces) in the South. In addition, the Navy's elite SEAL (Sea, Air, and Land) commando units carried out raids and **reconnaissance** missions in an effort to prevent the Viet Cong from receiving supplies.

Many people felt that the war was not managed well by U.S. politicians, and some Navy pilots were frustrated that they were not allowed to attack certain targets that were of far greater military value than those they were actually sent against. Although the Navy performed with great professionalism, U.S. public opinion soon turned against the war. By the end of the 1960s, it was

Below: An F-14 Tomcat prepares to launch from the carrier USS *John C. Stennis.* The Tomcat is carrying two laser-guided bombs under the fuselage and air-to-air missiles beneath its wings.

F-14 Tomcat

The F-14 Tomcat is a supersonic interceptor aircraft with two crew members. The Tomcat went on its first mission in 1975 and covered the evacuation of U.S. diplomats from Saigon, South Vietnam. From the early 1990s, F-14s were given the ability to drop bombs, and the airplane has been used as a strike fighter ever since. The Tomcat will be retired from service in 2008. It is perhaps most famous for appearing in the movie *Top Gun,* starring Tom Cruise.

clear that the United States would withdraw from Vietnam as soon as it could; this was achieved in 1973.

Technological Developments

While the Vietnam War was going on, the U.S. Navy also carried out its duties elsewhere in the world and made some major technological developments. Following the development of the atom bomb, scientists began investigating how nuclear power might be used in other ways. The Navy saw nuclear power as a potentially valuable means of propulsion for its ships and submarines, since it would enable them to travel great distances without the need to refuel. The leading supporter of nuclear power for the Navy was Admiral Hyman G. Rickover, who campaigned tirelessly on the issue in the years following World War II. He was rewarded when the submarine *Nautilus* entered service in 1955, demonstrating the validity of nuclear propulsion. The *Nautilus* was followed by a whole series of nuclear-powered submarines. The aircraft carrier *Enterprise*, commissioned in 1961, was built with nuclear power, and the later *Nimitz*-class carriers use a similar means of propulsion.

Above: The submarine USS *Nautilus* is seen here off New York City in October 1959. *Nautilus* was the first nuclear-powered submarine to join the U.S. Navy and became famous for sailing to the North Pole in 1958.

Race Issues in the Navy

The U.S. Navy has kept up with the times and now offers equal opportunities to ethnic minorities and women. African Americans have been part of the Navy since its creation, but their treatment has varied considerably. Initially, they were able to serve as enlisted men throughout the Navy, but by the 1900s, African Americans had been forced into menial jobs. African Americans were also segregated from their white colleagues. The first steps to change this situation occurred in 1942, when the Navy opened all enlisted posts to African Americans, although training and most service units remained racially **segregated**. Two years later, the first officers of African American origin joined the Navy. President Harry Truman ended racial segregation in the armed forces in 1948, the same year in which Ensign Jesse LeRoy Brown became the first African American naval aviator (he was later killed in Korea). The next year, Wesley A. Brown became the first African American to complete a Naval Academy education. Today, all positions in the Navy are open to men and women from all ethnic backgrounds.

Right: Ensign Jesse LeRoy Brown, the first African American naval aviator, is pictured in the cockpit of his Vought F4U Corsair.

The Navy also built up a large stockpile of nuclear weapons, many of them capable of being launched from nuclear-powered, ballistic-missile submarines against targets thousands of miles away. Having the awesome destructive power of nuclear weapons available was felt by some to be the best means of persuading the Soviet Union not to start a war with NATO. Fortunately, the awesome destructive power of the Navy's nuclear weapons was never called upon during the Cold War. Eventually, the Soviet Union collapsed, and the Cold War ended in 1991.

Women in the Navy

Women have played an important part in the U.S. Navy's history, but they served in a support capacity (often as nurses) for most of this time. Although the Equal Rights Amendment passed by Congress in 1972 was not **ratified**, the Department of Defense followed the spirit of the legislation and opened opportunities for women to serve throughout the Navy. The first women began flight training in 1973, and in 1976, the first female students attended the Naval Academy. Women were also assigned to surface ships. Although there were more opportunities, women could only serve in noncombat positions until the 1990s. In 1993, combat aviation positions began opening to female aircrews, and in 1994, the first women to join as surface combatants were posted to the aircraft carrier *Dwight D. Eisenhower*. Female pilots were involved in combat operations over Iraq in Operation Desert Fox in 1998 and have been involved in similar missions ever since.

Above: A Trident D5 submarine-launched ballistic missile is test-fired from the submarine *Tennessee*. The Trident is normally fitted with several nuclear warheads and forms part of the United States' nuclear arsenal.

Left: Quartermaster 1st Class Desiree Uebele is seen talking on a hand-held radio. As shown on her cap, she was assigned to the Naval Air Station at Key West, Florida, when this photograph was taken.

Chapter 5

The U.S. Navy Today

Right: An SH-60 Seahawk helicopter transfers cargo to the ammunition ship *Flint*. Helicopters are among the most versatile aircraft in navy service, being used for transportation, rescue, and anti-submarine warfare duties.

Although the Cold War was over, the U.S. Navy remained busy. On August 2, 1990, Iraqi dictator Saddam Hussein invaded Kuwait. The United States led the U.N.'s demands for Saddam to withdraw, but he refused. On January 17, 1991, the U.N. launched a massive assault to liberate Kuwait. U.S. Navy ships fired cruise missiles against a range of Iraqi targets, while carrier-based aircraft joined in the air assault on targets in Iraq and Kuwait. The air and missile war raged for six weeks before Saddam's army was defeated in a 100-hour-long ground war. Kuwait was liberated, but Saddam was still in power and was still a threat to his neighbors. Suspicions that he was attempting to develop weapons of mass destruction (WMD; nuclear, chemical, and biological weapons) remained. The Navy kept a watch on Saddam, launching carrier-based jets to help enforce "no-fly zones" over the north and south of Iraq, imposed to stop any activity by what remained of Saddam's air force. Cruisers, frigates, and destroyers made sure that merchant ships did not try to smuggle weapons and **contraband** goods to Iraq.

Below: A crew member of the submarine *Norfolk* looks through the periscope to scan the surface of the sea. The *Norfolk* was sailing off the coast of the former Yugoslavia at the time this photograph was taken.

Peacekeeping Efforts

The Navy spent much of the rest of the 1990s contributing to peacekeeping operations throughout the world, often using amphibious craft to send U.S. Marines ashore. Peacekeeping, however, was not the only role for the Navy, which saw more combat during the course of the decade. Evidence that Saddam Hussein had been involved in a plot to murder former President George H. W. Bush prompted President Bill Clinton to use the Navy to retaliate against Saddam by launching cruise missiles at targets in Iraq in 1996. This was followed two years later by a larger operation known as Operation Desert Fox. Carrier-based aircraft joined those in Kuwait to strike at targets associated with Iraq's WMD program. Then, in 1999, carrier-based aircraft and cruise missiles were used once more, this time against targets in Serbia. Serbian President Slobodan Milosevic had begun a campaign of **genocide** against ethnic Albanians living in Kosovo, and

The U.S. Naval Academy

In 1845, Secretary of the Navy George Bancroft set up the U.S. Naval Academy in Annapolis, Maryland. The Academy educates future officers for both the Navy and the Marine Corps and provides academic and professional training for students. The Academy places great importance on moral and ethical development, expecting students to show honor, integrity, and respect for their colleagues. This is coupled with a broad-based academic program that covers science, mathematics, engineering, and the humanities. Students spend four years at the Academy before they are assigned to their first posting.

after diplomatic efforts to stop the campaign failed, NATO launched an air assault on Serbia. The attack lasted for 78 days before Milosevic accepted NATO's terms.

The War on Terror

At the start of the twenty-first century, the United States' position as the world's only superpower was unchallenged. The Cold War was becoming a distant memory, and U.S. national security appeared assured. Then, on September 11, 2001, terrorists from Osama bin Laden's al-Qaeda network hijacked four airliners. Two were flown into the World Trade Center in New York City, another hit the Pentagon, and the fourth crashed in open countryside in Pennsylvania while the passengers heroically tried to overpower the terrorists. The world was stunned by the attacks, in which thousands of people were killed. The Navy was placed on alert and sent to defend the coastlines, while the armed forces watched over a shocked nation and President George W. Bush's administration sought to bring Osama bin Laden to justice. Bin Laden had been living in Afghanistan, and President Bush demanded that the government of Afghanistan, the Taliban, hand bin Laden over so that he could be put on trial. The Taliban refused, and President Bush sent U.S. troops into battle to remove al-Qaeda's strongholds in Afghanistan and to overthrow the Taliban. Once again, the Navy played a vital part in the campaign. Cruise missiles were fired against a variety of targets, while Navy airplanes provided air support. Within a matter of weeks, the Taliban had been ousted and Afghanistan was no longer a safe haven for al-Qaeda. Although the fate of Osama bin Laden is still uncertain as of this writing, there is little doubt that the United States' actions represented a setback for his terrorist operations, even if the threat posed by his organization remains.

The success in Afghanistan did not mark the end of the war on terror, however, and concerns grew that terrorists might seek to use WMD against the United States. President Bush's administration was particularly concerned that Saddam Hussein might be willing to provide such weapons to terrorists as an act of revenge. After the Persian Gulf War (1990–1991), the U.N. had demanded that Saddam stop all attempts at developing WMD and sent inspectors to enforce its requirements. It was not certain, however, that Saddam had ever stopped his development program, and fears remained that he still held some stocks of lethal nerve gas. Inspectors were sent again to investigate whether or not Saddam was continuing to develop such weapons, or whether he had actually produced any. Saddam did little to help the inspectors, and President Bush, supported by British Prime Minister Tony Blair, led calls for the U.N. to present Saddam with a choice: either cooperate properly with the inspectors, or the United States and Britain would lead efforts to disarm Iraq by force. Saddam Hussein ignored the demands, and President Bush decided to use military force, even though a number of countries did not agree with this decision. Operations began on March 21, 2003. Once again, Navy cruise missiles and aircraft played a major part in the campaign against Saddam. The Navy supported an amphibious landing on Iraq's Al Faw

Above: An E-2C Hawkeye early-warning aircraft lands aboard the carrier *Theodore Roosevelt* during Operation Iraqi Freedom in 2003. The Hawkeye carries a powerful radar in the dish mounted above the fuselage, which allows its crew to detect hostile airplanes.

Right: Sailors and Marines from the 13th Marine Expeditionary Unit provide humanitarian aid to Iraqi civilians during Operation Iraqi Freedom. The Marines rely upon Navy ships to carry them to war zones.

peninsula by British Royal Marines, using helicopters based on assault ships in the Arabian Gulf to fly the attacking forces ashore. Navy aircraft also attacked targets across Iraq as the war raced to a swift conclusion. U.S. troops took Iraq's capital, Baghdad, and on May 1, 2003, President Bush announced that major combat operations had ended. However, insurgent attacks on U.S. forces continued long after war had officially been declared over, and in time more U.S. troops died after the "end" of the war than before. Saddam Hussein went into hiding, but was captured by U.S. troops on December 14, 2003.

The Future

Saddam Hussein has been defeated, the Taliban has been removed from power, and Afghanistan is no longer considered a safe haven for al-Qaeda operations, but the world is far from stable. The threat from terrorism remains, while states seeking to arm themselves with WMD remain a major concern for the United States. The Navy remains a key part of the U.S. armed services and continues to adopt the latest technology. Computerization has been employed to reduce the number of sailors required to operate ships, while weapons become ever more accurate. A new carrier, the USS *George H.W. Bush*, will enter service in 2009, followed by a new generation of aircraft carriers, with new airplanes aboard them.

Left: Petty Officer Kandace Armstrong notes the status of aircraft flying from the carrier USS *John F. Kennedy* during Operation Enduring Freedom in 2002.

Right: The submarine USS *Seawolf* carries out sea trials before entering full service with the fleet. *Seawolf* is one of the most modern submarines in service and is equipped with a mixture of torpedoes and Tomahawk Land Attack Missiles.

During the Cold War, the two major weapons systems used by the Navy were the ballistic-missile submarine and the aircraft carrier. Now that the Cold War is over, the importance of having nuclear-armed submarines has diminished slightly, but the vessels themselves remain important. The submarines now used in this role are the Ohio-class, named after the first vessel of this design, USS *Ohio*. Ohio-class submarines are armed with twenty-four Trident ballistic missiles and conduct extended patrols, spending many weeks at a time beneath the waves. To reflect changing defense priorities, some of these submarines have had their Trident missiles replaced with Tomahawk cruise missiles. The submarines carry 154 of these weapons, making the craft extremely important strike platforms. They can be used to launch cruise missiles against land targets, hunt and sink enemy ships, or carry out reconnaissance. They are also able to transport Navy SEALs or other Special Forces soldiers.

There are currently twelve aircraft carriers in service. Ten of these are nuclear-propelled (nine Nimitz-class ships and the USS *Enterprise*), while the USS *Kitty Hawk* and the USS *John F. Kennedy* are steam-powered. The *Kitty Hawk* will be replaced in 2008, but the *Kennedy* will stay in use until 2017. Each carrier has around seventy airplanes. Vessels in the Navy's surface fleet are known as **cruisers**, destroyers, or frigates, depending on their size. A Carrier Battle Group usually consists of a mix of cruisers, destroyers, and supporting vessels such as oilers, protected by attack submarines.

The Navy also has a fleet of amphibious assault vessels, from which the U.S. Marines operate. These ships

U.S. Navy Bases in the United States

This map shows the locations of major U.S. Navy bases across the United States.

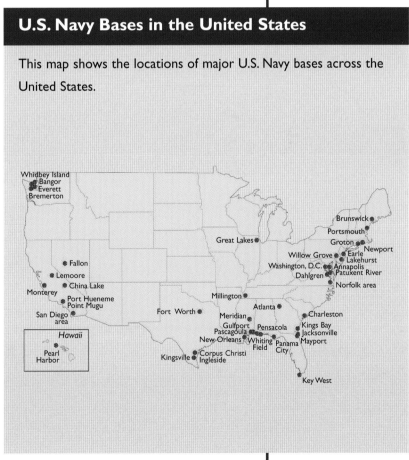

Carrier Air Wings

U.S. Navy aircraft carriers can **embark** up to 90 aircraft, but this makes the flight deck and hangar quite crowded. Normally, around 70 airplanes are embarked, though this figure varies, depending on the mission assigned to the carrier. If the carrier is given a task such as supporting Special Forces operations, it will carry fewer jets and more helicopters, to allow the troops to be carried ashore.

The normal complement of aircraft on a carrier today (known as an air wing) is around 50 strike fighter aircraft, made up of a mix of F-14s and F/A-18s (as the F/A-18 Super Hornet joins the fleet, the F-14 will be withdrawn). There are normally four E-2 Hawkeye radar-warning planes and a similar number of EA-6B Prowler electronic-warfare aircraft (these jam enemy radars and communications, and use HARM [High-Speed Anti-Radiation Missiles] missiles to attack radar sites). The S-3 Viking began life as an antisubmarine aircraft, but is now used as a refueling tanker and on patrol missions. Finally, there are a number of Seahawk helicopters used for antisubmarine and rescue duties. Uninhabited Air Vehicles (UAVs) possibly will be carried in the near future. These robot-controlled planes can carry out reconnaissance and attack missions. The United States leads the field in developing these craft.

Below: Seen here in the Atlantic Ocean in late 2003, the ships of the USS *George Washington* Carrier Battle Group sail in formation while training for their next deployment.

carry landing craft (often air-cushioned vehicles) and helicopters to carry troops and equipment ashore. To provide air support, these ships also embark a small number of AV-8B Harrier jets and AH-1W Super Cobra attack helicopters.

What does the Navy do with all this? The answer is that the basic duty of the Navy, to protect the United States, remains unchanged. Tasks such as protecting

F/A-18C Hornet and F/A-18E/F Super Hornet

The Hornet was designed as a single-seat multirole aircraft. It is used for fighter and attack missions, and some airplanes are modified to carry camera gear for reconnaissance operations. The first Hornets joined the Navy in the early 1980s and have seen action on many occasions. The basic Hornet design served as the basis for the Super Hornet, which looks similar to its smaller "brother." There are two main versions of the Super Hornet. The E-model is flown by just the pilot, while the F-model carries a Weapons System Operator as well. The Super Hornet will replace the F-14 in service.

Below: An F/A-18E Super Hornet takes off from the deck of the USS *Abraham Lincoln* during Operation Iraqi Freedom, the first major combat deployment for the Super Hornet.

U.S. Navy Bases Around the World

This map shows the locations of major U.S. Navy bases around the world.

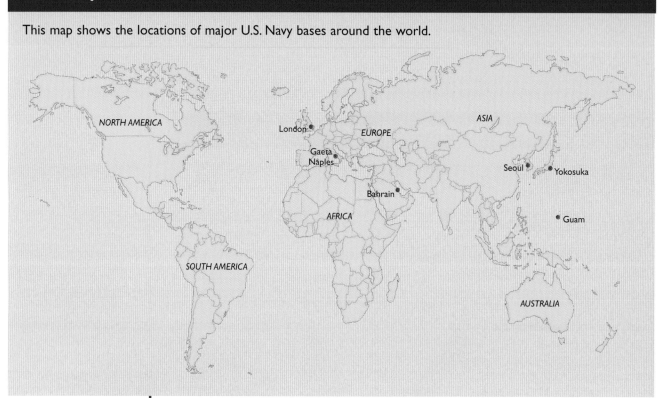

shipping and dealing with enemy ships would be familiar to John Paul Jones and Matthew Perry, although they would be amazed at the technology available to today's sailors. They would also recognize the responsibility of landing Marines on enemy-held shores to capture territory. Even attacking enemy land positions from the sea is an "old" mission. The difference now is that aircraft or missiles can be launched from Navy ships to attack targets hundreds of miles away. In addition to fighting wars, the Navy uses its ships to support humanitarian operations. These range from rescuing sailors from sinking ships, to taking food shipments to areas affected by famine, or aiding peacekeeping forces sent to nations that have been affected by civil war.

Although this chapter has concentrated on the ships and weapons of the Navy, it is important to remember that they would be useless without the highly trained, skilled, and dedicated personnel needed to operate and maintain them. The Navy's most important asset is its personnel, something that can often be forgotten

The Decline of the Battleship

Once the pride of the world's navies, the battleship fell out of favor after World War II, when its vulnerability to air attack meant that it ceased to be the most effective way of attacking enemy ships. As a result, battleship construction stopped, and the big ships began to be retired from service. However, the big guns carried by battleships were an extremely effective means of bombarding enemy positions from the sea, and the U.S. Navy decided to retain the four Iowa-class battleships. These were used in the Korean War, but after 1955, some of the class were placed in reserve. The *New Jersey* was used in Vietnam to provide fire support, but was then returned to the reserve.

Under President Ronald Reagan, the U.S. Navy underwent a large-scale expansion. Part of this led to the decision to return all four battleships to service after a modification program that fitted them with missiles as well as retaining their 16-inch guns. New Jersey was the first to see action, off Lebanon in 1983, and the *Wisconsin* and *Missouri* were used in operation Desert Storm. However, the cost of the ships, operating them, and finding enough sailors to crew them, led to the decision to withdraw them from use, this time for good, in 1992.

Left: Flight deck personnel work to stow one of the emergency barriers aboard the USS *Enterprise*. The barrier is used to stop aircraft that are unable to engage the arrestor wire system on the carrier's deck.

when our attention is drawn to the sleek airplanes and purposeful-looking ships and submarines. The U.S. Navy's 300,000 men and women are the key reason for the Navy's success, and it is important to remember that they are the real means through which the Navy defends the United States.

How Navy Ships Get their Names

It is traditional that ships (and now submarines) should have a name. The names of U.S. Navy ships come from a variety of sources. Many of today's vessels are named after famous ships from the history of the Navy (such as the *Enterprise*); American towns, cities, and states (the *Ohio*); battles (*Yorktown*); and famous individuals, especially those with connections to the Navy (*John Paul Jones*, *Nimitz*). Recent aircraft carriers, for example, have been named for U.S. presidents (the *Dwight D. Eisenhower*, *Abraham Lincoln*, *Ronald Reagan*) or politicians who supported the Navy in Congress (*Carl Vinson*, *John C. Stennis*). Although there are various types of ships, it is usual for more than one vessel of the same design to be built. All vessels of identical design (or which are minor modifications of the original design) are said to belong to a particular "class" of ships or submarines. The name of the class is normally taken from the first to be built. For example, submarines built to the same design as the USS *Ohio* are said to be Ohio-class submarines.

Right: The cruiser USS *Leahy* is seen underway. Named for Admiral William D. Leahy, the ship was the lead vessel in a class of guided missile cruisers. The ship entered service in 1962 and served for 31 years.

Left: Although the Navy's ships are equipped with the latest navigational equipment, there is still a use for old-fashioned manual items such as this sextant, used for calculating the ship's position.

Table of Ranks and Ratings

Rank	Grade	Rank	Grade
Fleet Admiral	O-11	Chief Warrant Officer 3	W-3
Admiral	O-10	Chief Warrant Officer 2	W-2
Vice-Admiral	O-9	Warrant Officer	W-1
Rear-Admiral (upper half)	O-8	Master Chief Petty Officer of the Navy	E-9
Rear-Admiral (lower half)	O-7	Master Chief Petty Officer	E-9
Captain	O-6	Senior Chief Petty Officer	E-8
Commander	O-5	Chief Petty Officer	E-7
Lieutenant-Commander	O-4	Petty Officer First Class	E-6
Lieutenant	O-3	Petty Officer Second Class	E-5
Lieutenant (Junior Grade)	O-2	Petty Officer Third Class	E-4
Ensign	O-1	Seaman	E-3
Chief Warrant Officer 5	W-5	Seaman Apprentice	E-2
Chief Warrant Officer 4	W-4	Seaman Recruit	E-1

Notes: The rank of Fleet Admiral is only awarded in wartime. The rank of Warrant Officer is no longer used by the Navy, but is included in this table for completeness.

Time Line

1775:	October 13: the first legislation of the Continental Congress regarding the Navy is passed; December 3: the first fleet of the Navy is put in commission.
1785:	The last ship of the Continental Navy is sold off.
1794:	Congress authorizes new ships for the Navy.
1798–1801:	The Undeclared War with France takes place.
1801–1805:	War with Barbary Pirates.
1812–1815:	War with Great Britain.
1861–1865:	Civil War.
1898:	War with Spain.
1914:	World War I breaks out in Europe.
1917:	April, United States enters World War I.
1918:	November 11, World War I ends.
1941:	December 7: Japanese attack Pearl Harbor.
1942–1945:	U.S. forces advance toward Japan.
1945:	May, Germany surrenders; August, Japan surrenders.
1950–1953	Korean War.
1964:	Air strikes against targets in Vietnam from Navy carriers.
1975:	The Navy covers the withdrawal of American citizens from Saigon in Vietnam.
1990:	Saddam Hussein invades Kuwait.
1991:	Gulf War; Iraq is defeated.
2001:	Terrorist attacks on U.S.; Navy planes and missiles attack terrorist targets in Afghanistan.
2003:	Operation Iraqi Freedom; U.S. Navy participates in removal of Saddam Hussein from power.

Glossary

atrocity: an act that is extremely wicked, cruel, or brutal

blockade: the isolation by a warring nation of an enemy area by troops or warships to prevent the passage of persons or supplies

communist: someone who believes in a system in which goods are owned in common and are available to all as needed

contraband: goods or merchandise whose importation, exportation, or possession is forbidden by the government

cruiser: a large, fast, moderately armored and gunned warship

democracy: a system of government by the whole population of voting age, usually through elected representatives

destroyer: a small, fast warship used especially to support larger vessels and usually armed with five-inch guns, depth charges, torpedoes, and often guided missiles

dictatorship: a form of government in which absolute power is concentrated in one person

economy: a system of producing and distributing goods and services

embark: to go or be carried on board a ship for transportation

emigrate: to leave one's place of residence or country to live elsewhere

frigate: a warship that is smaller than a destroyer

genocide: the deliberate and systematic destruction of a racial, political, or cultural group

guerrilla: a person who engages in irregular warfare especially as a member of an independent unit carrying out harassment and sabotage

mutiny: an organized revolt (as of a naval crew) against discipline or a superior officer

ratify: to formally approve

reconnaissance: an exploratory military survey of enemy territory

segregate: to set apart from others or from the general population

Further Information

Books:

Abramovitz, Melissa. *The U.S. Navy at War.* Mankato, MN: Capstone Press, 2001.

Bledsoe, Glen and Karen E. Bledsoe. *The Blue Angels: The U.S. Navy Flight Demonstration Squadron.* Mankato, MN: Capstone Press, 2001.

Graham Gaines, Ann. *The Navy in Action.* Berkeley Heights, NJ: Enslow Publishers, Inc., 2001.

McNab, Chris. *Protecting the Nation with the U.S. Navy.* Philadelphia: Mason Crest Publishers, 2003.

Payment, Simone. *Navy SEALs: Special Operations for the U.S. Navy.* New York: Rosen Publishing Group, 2003.

Web sites:

U.S. Navy's Official Web Site
   www.navy.mil/
   This is the home page for the U.S. Navy.

Navy Fact File
   www.chinfo.navy.mil/navpalib/factfile/ffiletop.html
   This site provides information on Navy ships, submarines, and airplanes.

How Navy Ships Get Their Names
   www.history.navy.mil/faqs/faq63-1.htm
   This website explains in detail how ships are named.

Navy.com
   www.navy.com/index.jsp
   Interested in the Navy as a career? This site is a great place to start gathering information.

Officer Training Command Pensacola
   www.nsgreatlakes.navy.mil/otcp/
   This site provides information on the Navy's Officer Training schools.

DefenseLINK
   www.defenselink.mil/
   This is the official site for the Department of Defense.

Index

Page numbers in **bold** indicate
photographs or illustrations

Abraham Lincoln, **39**
Afghanistan, 32
African Americans, 28
aircraft carriers, **18**, 18, 21, **25, 26,** 27,
 29, **33,** 35, **35,** 37, **38**, 38, **41**
airplanes,
 5, 17, **18**, **25**, **26**, **28**, **33**, 38, **39**, 39
Alfred, **6**
Allies, the, 20
al-Qaeda, 32
amphibious assault vehicles, 37
Annapolis Naval Academy, 13, **32**
Armstrong, Kandace, **35**
Arnold, Benedict, **7**, 8

bin Laden, Osama, 32
Birmingham, **18**, 18
Blair, Tony, 33
Bonhomme Richard, **8**, 9
British colonies, 5
British Marines, 34
British Royal Navy, 8, **8**, 9, **11**, 12, **13**, 17
Brown, Jesse LeRoy, **28**
Brown, Wesley A., 28
Bush, George W., 32, 33

China, 24
Churchill, Winston, 19
Civil War, 12–14
Clinton, Bill, 31
Cold War, 23, 29
Columbus, Christopher, 5
communism, 23, 25
Confederate Navy, 12, **14**
Constitution, **4**, **11**
Continental Navy, **7**, 11
Covington, **19**
Cuban independence, 14–15, **15**

Decatur, Stephen, **10**
Dwight D.Eisenhower, 29

Ely, Eugene, 18
Enterprise, 27, **41**

Flint, **30**
France, 5, 8, 11–12

George H.W. Bush, 35
George Washington, **38**
German Navy, 17, 20
Great Depression, 19

helicopters, **30**, 38
Hornet, 21
humanitarian missions, **34**, 40

Inchon, Battle of, 24
Iraq, 29, 31, **33**, 33–34, **34**, **39**

Japan, 12, 20
John C. Stennis, **26**
John F. Kennedy, **35**, 37
Johnson, Lyndon, 25
Jones, John Paul, 9, 40

Kitty Hawk, 37
Korean War, 23–24, 41
Kosovo, 31
Kuwait, 31

Lake Erie, Battle of, **13**
Lawrence, **13**
Leahy, **42**
Lebanon, 41
Lend-Lease, 19–20

Maddox, 25
Maine, 14, 15
Marianas Islands, 21
McKinley, William, 17
Midway, Battle of, 20, 21
Milosevic, Slobodan, 31–32
Missouri, **24**, 41

NATO (North Atlantic Treaty
  Organization), 23, 32
Nautilus, 27, **27**
neutrality, 19
New Jersey, 41
Niagara, **13**
Norfolk, **31**
nuclear power, 27, **27**
nuclear weapons, **29**, 29

Operation Desert Fox, 29, 31
Operation Desert Storm, 41
Operation Enduring Freedom, **35**
Operation Iraqi Freedom,
  33, 33–34, **34**, **39**
Oriskany, **25**

peacekeeping, 31–32
Pearl Harbor attacks, 20
Perry, Matthew, 12, 13, **13**, 40
Persian Gulf War, 31, 41
Philadelphia, **10**
Philippine independence, 14–15
pirates, **10**, 11
privateers, 7
Pusan, Battle of, 23

Quasi-War, 11–12

Ramage, **4**
Reagan, Ronald, 41
Revolutionary War, 5, **6**, 7–9
Rickover, Hyman G., 27
Roosevelt, Franklin D., **19**–20
Roosevelt, Theodore, **17**

Saddam Hussein, 31, 33
SEALs, **22**, 26, 37
Seawolf, **36**
Serbia, 31
sextants, **43**
Soviet Union, 23
Spanish colonies, 5
Spanish-American War, 14–15

Special Forces, 38
submarines, 5, 37
  U-boats, 17, 20

Tennessee, **29**
terrorism, 32–35
Theodore Roosevelt, **33**
Top Gun (movie), **26**
Truman, Harry S., 28

UAVs (Uninhabited Air Vehicles), 38
Uebele, Desiree, **29**
Union Navy, 12
United Nations, 23, 31, 33
United States independence, 11
United States Marine Corps, **34**
United States Navy, 7, **16**
  apprenticeships, 13
  bases, *37*, *40*
  engineer corps, 13
  ranks and ratings, 43
  special forces, **22**
  technological developments, 27, 29

Valcour Island, Battle of, 8
Vietnam War, 24–27
Virginia, **14**

War of 1812, **11**, 12, **13**
weapons, **29**, **36**, 37, 38, **42**
weapons of mass destruction (WMD),
  31, 33
Wilson, Woodrow, 17
Wisconsin, 41
women, 29
World Trade Center attacks, 32
World War I, 17–19
World War II, 19–21

Yorktown, Battle of, 11